folk tales from India

THE SUNDERBANS

Vol.1

Compiled by **Saswat Ghosh**
Illustrated by **Dipankar Bhattacharya**

VIVALOK COMICS

myths, legends and folk tales

For those who want to make sense of the world we are in, myths, legends and folk tales offer rich cultural resources of existential help. These three different genres can be grouped under the larger umbrella of 'folklore'. According to the well-known folklorist, A.K.Ramanujan, "wherever people live there is folklore."

Myths are not about gods and goddesses as they are normally perceived to be. They deal with impossible life situations that are part of the human predicament. Accidents, unnatural births and deaths, nature's fury, the relationship between character and destiny, good and evil, conflicts in unjust societies, human action and supernatural designs, origin of events, places, objects, species and ideas about the cosmos, are some of the recurrent themes of Indian myths. Given the intensity of such themes, only gods and goddesses can sometimes unravel these formidable issues. Pan Indian myths share ritual and festival calendars with highly varying regional, local and village temple myths. Major Indian festivals, belief systems, temple ceremonies, life cycle ceremonies, ritual components and behavioural patterns within rituals depend on what myths say. The major corpus of pan Indian Hindu myths contains eighteen major divisions, and their millions of variations and versions have led to the creation of exquisite temple architecture, stone and bronze sculptures, music and dance. Jain and Buddhist myths also have a pan Indian character with regional variations in architecture, sculpture, ritual and life cycle ceremonies. Indian tribal myths address the same set of issues but they do not share anything with the pan Indian myths.

Legends are historical chronicles, not necessarily authenticated, of local heroes, antiheroes and their heroic deeds. The local heroes of legends could be bandits, chieftains, caste and clan leaders and their heroic deeds could be winning a local battle or getting a cowherd from a rival group. Indian legends normally contain detailed descriptions of local geography, infusing places with historical meaning. Forts, monuments, gathering places, courses of rivers, mysteries of thick forests, mountain terrains, secret spots in the ocean, navigating the deserts, animal behavior and man's struggles against nature, form the corpus of Indian legends. The heroic values embedded in the legends are often communicated through various folk forms, and over a long passage of time legends blur into myths.

Folk tales are about everyday life. Mundane, earthy and honest negotiations that they are, their meanings are best found in their original contexts. The telling of a tale warrants a situation. Situations create versions of tales. So any tale at any given point is always retold. With every retelling, tales travel - across generations, languages and regions. They are like floating magic carpets which entertain, educate, fret, fume, take vengeance or amuse. They reveal politics of kinship and inter-community relationships in a particular region. We learn the natures of mothers, fathers, brothers, various in-laws, sons, daughters and grand parents from folk tales much more than contemporary psychology would reveal. Through folk tales we understand the roles of brahmins, fakirs, sadhus, astrologers, magicians, kings, clowns, fairies and genies and various animals. Could we have made sense of the world in this manner without folk tales? Folk tales also generate proverbs and riddles.

It is important to understand the general functions of myths, legends and folk tales in our society so that we appreciate their particular contexts. The ultimate challenge is not about making folklore accessible but it is about making 'folklore in context' accessible to audiences. And that is what this series intends to do.

M.D.Muthukumaraswamy.
National Folklore Support Centre, Chennai
The NFSC is dedicated to the promotion of Indian folklore research, training, networking and publications.

the world of comics

Comics is often thought of as the joining of two art forms: writing and drawing. But what happens between the panels isn't about either, it's the author's imagination.'

Scott McCloud, Understanding Comics

Comics are visual narratives which successfully tap the unexplored realms of imagination among all its readers, children and adult alike.

Comics have had a turbulent history so far. Besides raising the value of imagination and proclaiming the triumph of the good and the beautiful, they have also faced accusations of being frivolous, unclean, dark and negative. But that would be a criticism of the content and not the medium. Comics have been indomitably resilient and have a way of rising from the ashes every time they have been proclaimed dead! What's kept them alive are their sheer reading pleasure and their place as social commentators, mixing information with imagination. Their relevance, equally to young and old, cannot be denied.

The medium defies the logical style of narration and provides scope for broadened horizons and unlimited perceptions. Which of us has been left unaffected by the magical world of superheroes — Batman, Superman, Captain America and Mandrake the Magician? Or the mischief of Dennis the Menace, the cynicism of Calvin, the laziness of Garfield, the confrontations between the Romans and a group of Gauls led by Asterix, or the adventures of Tintin? The list is endless. We all have mentally mimicked the world of these characters, which though unreal, provided an insight into the real world.

Comics are now viewed as the unfolding of alternative spaces. From 1865, when the first comic strip *Max und Mortiz* was introduced in German papers, upto the 1960's, which experienced a 'dark' phase in comic history, this art form has covered many milestones. Besides projecting a lopsided and humorous view of life through lovable and unforgettable characters, it raised issues on terrorism, human rights, anarchism, racism and sexual politics. Art Speigelman's legendary holocaust creation, *Maus*, shook the world and won the Pulitzer Prize.

It was in the US that the comic form flourished. Joe Sacco, another legend, catapulted comics into the mainstream definition of acceptable reading. *The Times* published his strips regularly. But it was Robert Crumb who initiated and popularised a whole new genre in comics- 'underground comics'. He did a lifetime of work on the American way of life. His (much too) honest depiction of reality and his subversive brand of humour won him as many accolades as criticism.

According to McCloud, comics, or story telling through visuals, have an older history than what is commonly believed. He says, "Comics is about three thousand years old and maybe as old as art itself." Some examples, though they adopted a different style, are ancient Egyptian wall paintings on domes and the walls of ancient Indiantemples, such as the murals of Kerala.

Over five hundred years ago, there were European broadsheets that were more contemporary in form and narrated events in pictures. European comics were the first to make an impression and each nation had its own little term of endearment for the comic. In France, they used the term 'BDs' or 'Bandes Dessinee', as a term for drawn strips. The Italians called them 'fumetti' or 'little smokes' because the blurbs looked like little smoke clouds.

It was from France, however, that the next International comic wave began. Georges Remi's *Tintin* and Goscinny and Uderzo's group of indomitable Gauls led by Asterix, Obelix and Getafix the Druid, hit the readers' imagination in such a way as to give a whole new meaning to comics. The Europeans also blazed a new trail in science fiction and historical portrayals.

Almost parallel to these developments in comics was the evolution of Japanese comics ('Manga'). The emergence of Tetsuwan Atom (1951) created by Tezuka set the ball rolling with one of the best loved science fiction comics with a robot like character. This interesting representation of a super hero who fought for peace is best known as 'Astro Boy'. Apart from science fiction, Japanese comics lent themselves well to thrillers and underground comics. In the 80's Kiji Nakazawa's General of Hiroshima, a vivid, thought provoking autobiographical work once again brought out the maturity of style in the Japanese Manga.

In the Indian context, comics are but a logical continuation of the strong pictorial and narrative tradition that it already has. The *'pata chitras'* or scroll paintings of Bengal and the *'phad* of Rajasthan' exemplify this. Both these techniques combine the excitement of both the oral and visual form of story telling. Anant Pai who started the *Amar Chitra Katha* series made the first successful foray in this domain. Comics, he proved, were worthy of narrating sacred epics like the *Mahabharata*, the *Ramayana* and other mythological tales. In the sixties and seventies, *Indrajal Comics* brought to the Indian doorstep almost every favourite comic world character.

Today, there is a growing movement of comic book lovers who are trying to inject new life into this wonderful art form.

The Sundarbans,

The Sundarbans is the evergreen forest belt stretched across the large estuarine delta of the river Ganga. Covering 10,000 square kilometres, this unique mangrove forest lies across both India and Bangladesh down to the Bay of Bengal. The Sundarbans is a combination of wetlands and jungle, and includes fifty-four islands characterised by high salinity and changing land forms. As the Ganga splits into numerous creeks and channels like the roots of a banyan tree, the forests float, and in this dramatic play between mud and water, land gets re-sculpted. In fact, this area undergoes such intense, water-induced transformation that it needs to be re-mapped every three years!

Once upon a time, 24 Paraganas, the epicentre of the present Sundarbans was called 'Bhatir Desh' where the downstream river flows southwards, where ebb and tide sets the tune of the life of its inhabitants. This area lay on the other side of the international border, in what is now Bangladesh. The land was called Byaghratati. *'Byaghra'* means tiger and *'tati'*, seashore.

The story of the Sundarbans is a chronicle of the systematic and continual reclamation of jungles and their transformation into wet paddy fields, starting with the advent of the Turks and the Mughals, right into the British period. There was thus a steady migration of wet-rice cultivating communities - mostly Islamic - into previously forested areas. Holy men, popularly endowed with charismatic authority and a Sufi identity such as pirs and fakirs, played a pivotal role in this process, waging a ceaseless struggle against jungle and tiger. Indeed, Bengal is the only region where agriculture is associated in popular memory with the lives of Sufis. As loyalty to these pioneer saints or saint developers became channeled into stable cults, their graves, their descendants and their religious ideology became rooted among local communities as did Islam. Some of these pirs became legendary and were believed to possess occult powers. They are also associated with mosques, thereby institutionalising Islam. The pir's natural authority and patronage lay with the grass roots of Bengali society, and theirs in turn rarely extended beyond their local holy man.

Many of the stories in this volume are about taming the forest, in which the local holy men and women play a prominent role. The ferocity of the forest is symbolised by the Royal Bengal Tiger, though crocodiles, pythons and many other wild beasts cannot be overlooked. The Sundarban tigers are known to lurk beneath the mangrove roots and claim their prey by entering the water as fishing boats pass by! Praying to 'ma' or Banbibi, Goddess of the forest, precedes each foray into the jungle. Woodcutters, honey collectors, fishermen and boatmen who survive by the bounty of the forest, need these god-heroes who weave a mystical protective force that

where the royals roam...

saves each one from untold horrors.

These stories bring to the reader the most popular legends, myths and folktales of the region - fishermen and dalits who struggle to worship their favourite Goddess Bishalakshmi, Manik Pir who could cure all manner of diseases and who favours the just and punishes the greedy; Bada Khan Ghazi, the warrior saint and his love for a Hindu woman; Banbibi and her amicable settlement of dispute with Dakshin Ray, The Lord of Tigers and so on. They represent the vivacious imaginations of those who have to confront the vagaries of nature on a daily basis, merging the sacred and the everyday into an inextricable reality.

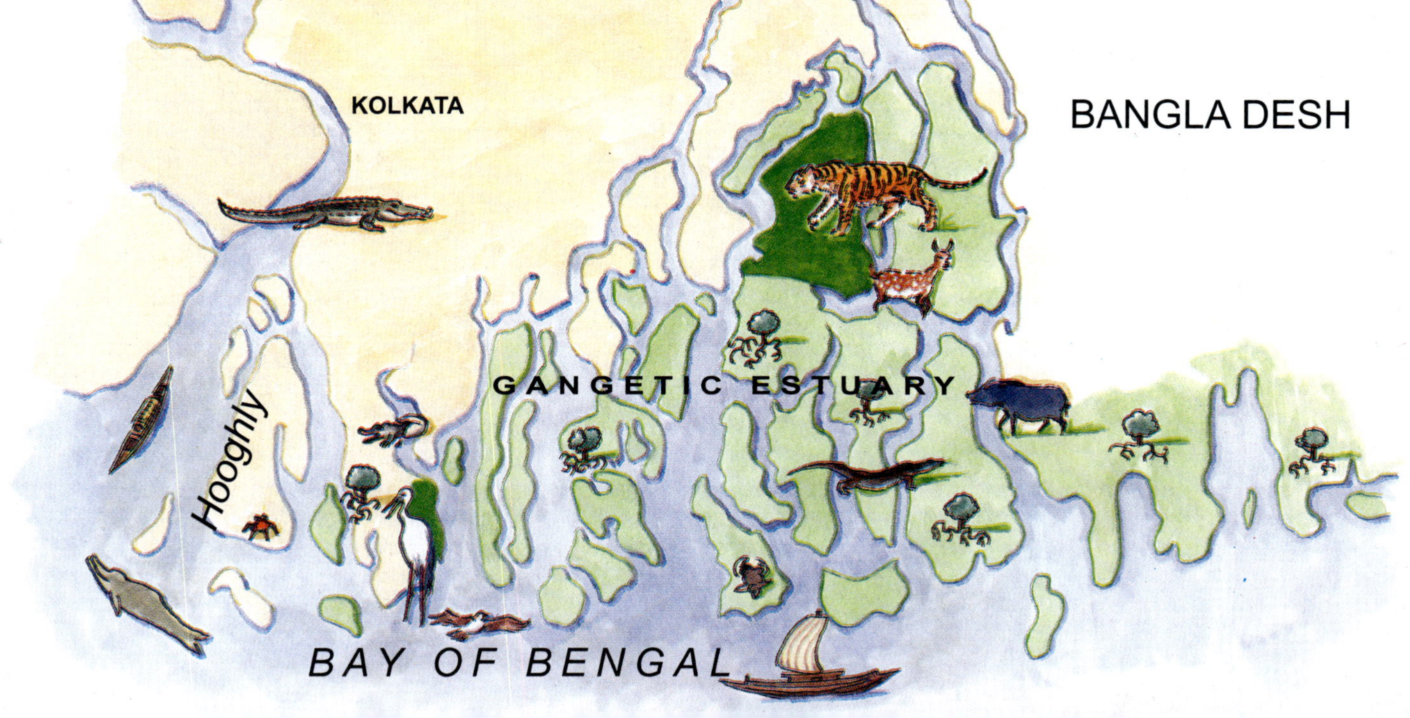

MEET THEM INSIDE!

heroes and gods of the Sunderbans

Manik Pir

The land of the Sunderbans In lower Bengal resonates with the stories of Manik Pir. Some of these stories are sung as Pala songs and are part of the piruli tradition. This word may have been derived from the two words *'pir'* and *'ali'* which mean a Muslim saint. Interestingly, pirulis are found among all communities including Brahmins. This clearly shows the harmonious intermingling of Hindu and Muslim cultures. In fact, the fertile culture of lower Bengal always nurtured a peaceful existence between religions. Manik Pir symbolises this mixed culture. Manik Pir is worshipped on both sides of the border (the other side of the border is now Bangladesh) as a patron of cows and guardian of diseases. There are many *dargahs* of Manik Pir in the 24 South Parganas district. People from far and near come to these *dargahs* with offerings. They bring *hazot*, which is milk from a recently calved cow. The stories of Manik Pir are part of the popular lore of the Sunderbans.

Bada Khan Ghazi

In 24 Parganas, the story of Bada Khan Ghazi is immensely popular. *Dargahs* dedicated to him are found in many places there.

Though the Ghazis are supposed to be warrior-preachers, Bada Khan Ghazi is more famous as a folk god who could cure deadly diseases such as madness, vomiting of blood, leprosy and broken bones. His name cannot be found in Muslim religious history he is adored more as a folk god and a local hero than as a historical figure. Those who go into the jungles to collect wood and honey pray to him before they start so that they are protected from the uncertainties of the deadly jungle. His devotees are mainly lower caste Hindus. Many of them had converted to Islam a long time ago. Later, when organised Islam stopped this tradition, they continued to worship these folk gods. Thus the myth of Bada Khan Ghazi survives in both the communities of lower Bengal.

Banbibi

The *Bibima* cult is part of the mother goddess tradition. She is a local goddess like many others found in India. Banbibi is worshipped in the Sundarbans for protection against the fierce animals of the jungle.

The name Banbibi is derived from the word 'ban' which means forest and 'bibi' which means sister. Unlike other folk gods and goddesses, Banbibi is not conceived as a protector of diseases. Her special powers protect and control the Bengal tiger. Naturally, Banbibi is worshipped by those who enter the jungle to collect wood (*kathure*), honey (*moule*), medicinal plants and other produce.

Banbibi has a following amongst both Hindus and Muslims. Muslim *fakirs* and *aulias* who wandered in the Sundarbans, preaching their cult, took her for a sister.

Bishalakshmi

Though worshipped in other regions as well, the cult of Bishalakshmi is predominant in the Sundarbans. The image of Bishalakshmi, as well as the rituals involved in her worship, indicate the influence of a prehistoric tribal cult. This cult is predominantly followed by lower caste Hindus, particularly in fishing communities by both fishermen and boatmen.

The story of Bishalakshmi shows how the *antyajas*[1] of Bengal lost their original gods and goddesses and with them, their folk religion too, due to the dominance and aggression of puranic Hinduism. The process of sanskritisation took place either by force or by persuasion, and this is clearly reflected in two episodes, which surround the myth related to a Bishalakshmi temple at Kantabeniya, near Karanjalee in the Sundarban area.

1. People from the lower caste.

The Birth of Manik Pir
IN A LITTLE VILLAGE LONG TIME AGO, KAMIRUDDIN AND HIS WIFE HIRA WERE BLESSED WITH TWO BEAUTIFUL CHILDREN, MANIK AND GAJ.
THEY SOUGHT THE HELP OF DUDHBIBI, A WET NURSE.
SUCH BEAUTIFUL CHILDREN DIDI!
YES, OF COURSE DUDHBIBI!
WHAT DO YOU THINK? AFTER ALL THEY ARE MY CHILDREN! WHAT ELSE DO YOU EXPECT OF ME? DON'T THE GRAINS DEPEND ON THE FIELD?
ALLAH THE ALL-KNOWING HEARD HER WORDS.
Oh! what vainglorious creatures these mortals be! Such vanity can't go unpunished! Jibrail! Come down at once and curse this vain woman!
HIRA FAINTED. KAMIRUDDIN WAS FURIOUS.
WHAT NONSENSE! I AM GOING TO GET RID OF THIS CURSE AND SAVE MY CHILDREN!
OH! MA

NO YOU ARE NOT, YOU ARROGANT MAN! DUDHBIBI, TAKE THESE CHILDREN, LOVE THEM, BRING THEM UP AS YOUR OWN AND MAKE THEM INTO FINE YOUNG MEN.
HI ALLAH!
DUDHBIBI FOLLOWED ALLAH'S INSTRUCTIONS.
WHAT SWEET BOYS! ALLAH HAS BEEN KIND...BUT HOW WILL I BRING THEM UP WITH SO MANY MOUTHS TO FEED ALREADY?
THE VILLAGE CARPENTER, BADAR ZENDA'S EYES FOLLOWED HER.
MAYBE ALLAH HIMSELF WILL SHOW ME THE WAY!
HO HO HUM!
HEY MY PRETTY ONE, WHY SO FAST?
LET'S SEE WHAT'S IN THAT BUNDLE?
WHAT'S IT TO YOU BADAR? CAN'T A WOMAN CARRY WHAT SHE WANTS WITHOUT HAVING TO WARD OFF YOUR PRYING EYES?
SWISH!
IN A FLASH BADAR REMOVED THE SWADDLING CLOTH THAT COVERED THE BABIES.
IT'S A BABY! WHOSE IS IT, YOU SLUT! AH, THERE ARE TWO OF THEM!

HAI ALLAH! WHAT OBSCENITIES! YOU SILLY MAN, THIS IS ALLAH'S GIFT TO ME. THESE ANGELS ARE GOING TO BE MY SONS.
YOUR SONS!? DON'T YOU HAVE ENOUGH MOUTHS TO FEED ALREADY? YOU ARE BUT A MAID AND SO POOR THAT YOU DON'T EVEN EARN SEVEN RUPEES A MONTH. HERE, GIVE THEM TO ME!
HOW CAN I GIVE YOU WHAT ALLAH HAS GIVEN ME?
YOU WILL WHEN YOU SEE THIS! LOOK, YOU DON'T EVEN EARN THIS MUCH IN A WHOLE MONTH. HOW ABOUT A RED SARI AND BANGLES, AND A FINE DHOTI FOR YOUR MAN?
HE HE!
WAVE WAVE
DUDHBIBI WEIGHED THE SITUATION...
...TOOK THE TEN RUPEES, GAVE THE BUNDLE TO BADAR AND HASTENED HOME GUILTILY.
BADAR AND HIS WIFE CHURATBIBI WERE CHILDLESS. THE TWO BOYS, MANIK AND GAJ WERE BROUGHT UP AS THEIR OWN CHILDREN.
SOON AFTER, BADAR ZENDA LEFT HOME FOR MANY YEARS.
THE BOYS WERE GROWING UP...

BADAR RETURNED AFTER SEVERAL YEARS.
ON COMING HOME...
SOMEONE IN MY WIFE'S BED !!?
THIS IS WHAT YOU DO WHEN I AM NOT HERE! YOUR LOVER IS GOING TO PAY FOR THIS WITH HIS LIFE!
YOU SHAMELESS HUSSY!
THAK
YOU ARE COMPLETELY WRONG. IT'S NOT WHAT YOU THINK, DON'T ACT IN HASTE! YOU'LL REGRET IT, YOU WILL!

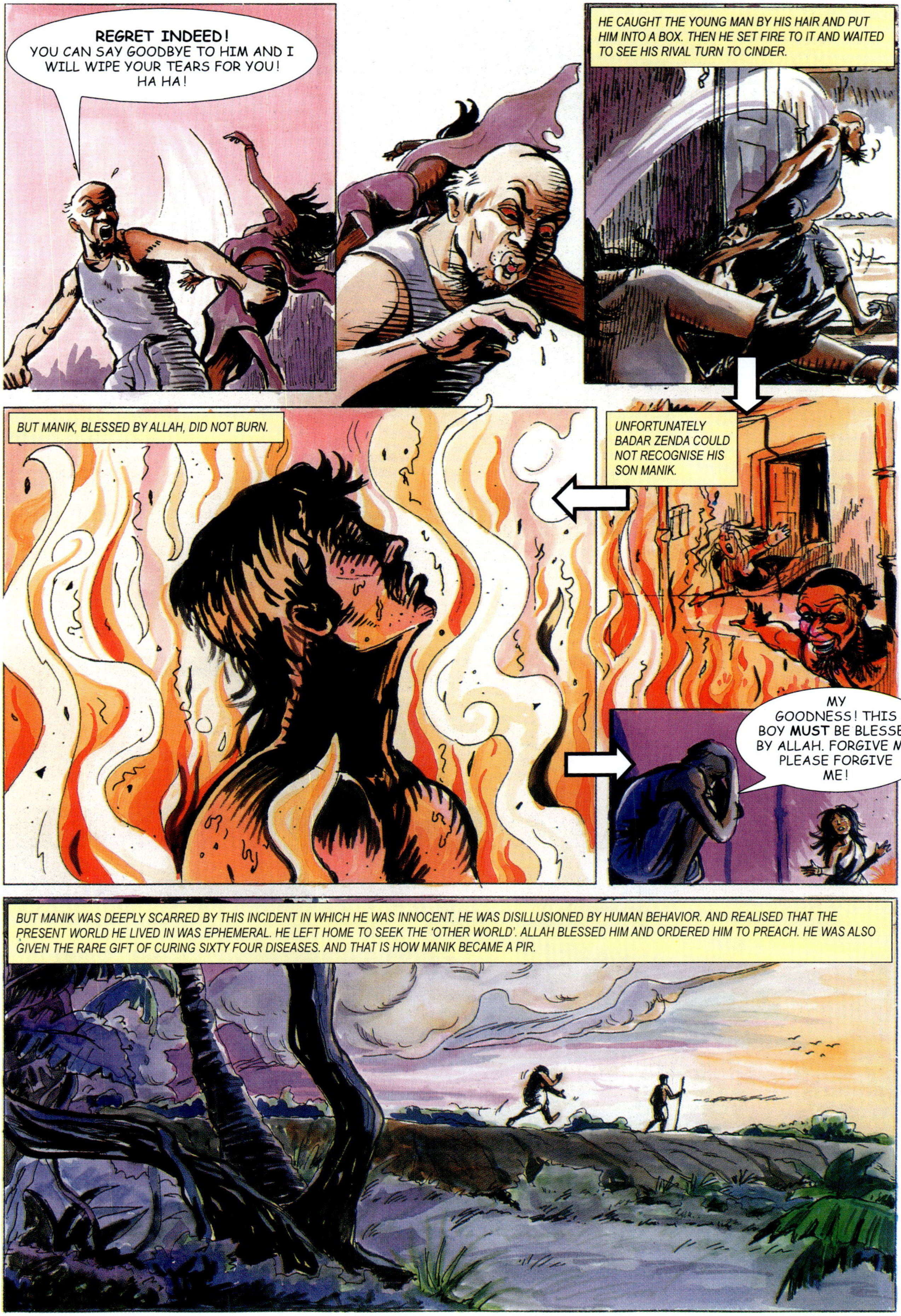

REGRET INDEED!
YOU CAN SAY GOODBYE TO HIM AND I WILL WIPE YOUR TEARS FOR YOU! HA HA!
HE CAUGHT THE YOUNG MAN BY HIS HAIR AND PUT HIM INTO A BOX. THEN HE SET FIRE TO IT AND WAITED TO SEE HIS RIVAL TURN TO CINDER.
UNFORTUNATELY BADAR ZENDA COULD NOT RECOGNISE HIS SON MANIK.
BUT MANIK, BLESSED BY ALLAH, DID NOT BURN.
MY GOODNESS! THIS BOY MUST BE BLESSED BY ALLAH. FORGIVE ME, PLEASE FORGIVE ME!
BUT MANIK WAS DEEPLY SCARRED BY THIS INCIDENT IN WHICH HE WAS INNOCENT. HE WAS DISILLUSIONED BY HUMAN BEHAVIOR. AND REALISED THAT THE PRESENT WORLD HE LIVED IN WAS EPHEMERAL. HE LEFT HOME TO SEEK THE 'OTHER WORLD'. ALLAH BLESSED HIM AND ORDERED HIM TO PREACH. HE WAS ALSO GIVEN THE RARE GIFT OF CURING SIXTY FOUR DISEASES. AND THAT IS HOW MANIK BECAME A PIR.

THE END

1. *Give us something*

HO HO ! HA HA ! CURD MIXED WITH COW'S URINE. HOW ABOUT THAT! GIVE ME MORE THEY WILL SAY... HEE HEE !
BUT MANIK PIR WITH HIS PSYCHIC POWERS COULD SEE THE CONTENTS OF THE VESSEL AS CLEAR AS DAYLIGHT.
MOTHER, WHY DO YOU SERVE US THIS IMPURE CURD ?
HMMPH ! WHY DON'T YOU SHOW ME HOW TO MILK A COW WHEN SHE IS INFERTILE, YOU CHEEKY MAN ?
I WILL, IF THAT'S WHAT YOU WANT.
MAGICALLY, MANIK DREW SEVEN POTS OF MILK FROM THE COW.
SANAKA SATI, HIRE'S SOFT-HEARTED DAUGHTER-IN-LAW WAS WATCHING...
WHEN WILL SHE CHANGE HER WAYS ? WILL WE STARVE IF WE GIVE AWAY A POT OF MILK ?
TRYING TO BE CLEVER, YOU CHEEKY BEGGAR ?
NOT A DROP OF MILK WILL YOU GET ! HARI, O HARI, COME AND PICK UP THESE POTS BEFORE THESE WASTRELS DO !
BUT IT WAS TOO LATE...
OH PIR BABA, HERE IS SOME MILK. I ASK FOR FOR-GIVENESS ON BEHALF OF MY MOTHER -IN-LAW.
KIND LADY, MAY YOU NEVER BECOME A WIDOW AND HAVE A BROKEN HEART.
NEVER FEAR, WE WILL APPEAR BEFORE YOU IF YOU EVER NEED US.
HIRE RUBBED HER HANDS IN GLEE. A NEW PLOT FORMED IN HER HEAD. WHEN KINU CAME IN...
KINU, MY SON, HAS OUR HOUSEHOLD EVER BEEN SULLIED BY THE PRESENCE OF OTHER COMMUNITIES ? TODAY, THE UNSPEAKABLE HAS HAPPENED. YOUR DEVOTED HINDU WIFE WAS TOUCHED BY A MUSLIM !

MADDENED WITH RAGE, KINU PICKED UP A STICK AND RAINED BLOWS ON POOR SANAKA.
WHAT MAN IS HE THAT WOULD DARE LAY A HAND ON HIS WIFE? DOES RAGE MAKE A MAN SO BLIND THAT HE LOSES CONTROL OVER HIMSELF? WHAT MAKES YOU MORE UPSET, THAT HE WAS A MUSLIM OR A MAN?
HEAR ME FIRST. THEY WERE FAKIRS. I GAVE THEM SOME MILK. THEY BLESSED ME AND TOUCHED MY HEAD. THEY ARE STILL WALKING THROUGH OUR VILLAGE.
KINU CHARGED TOWARDS THEM LIKE A RAGING BULL
STILL IN THE VILLAGE EH?. I'LL SHOW THEM!
STOP! HAVE SOME RESPECT FOR THE HOLY MEN.
HOW DARE YOU COME TO MY HOUSE AND TOUCH MY GOOD HINDU WIFE!
I WILL... AAAHHH! OOH...
YOUNG MAN, A BLESSING HAS NO RELIGION OR COMMUNITY. AND IT IS NOT MALE OR FEMALE.
SUDDENLY KINU'S HANDS WENT NUMB AND HIS BODY BEGAN TO BREAK OUT IN PUSTULES
WHO DO YOU THINK YOU ARE? YOU THINK YOU CAN SCARE ME WITH THESE PUSTULES!?
BUT KINU HAD BECOME A LEPER!
DESPERATE, KINU ROSE TO STRIKE ANOTHER BLOW. BUT A DEADLY SNAKE APPEARED AND BIT HIM ON HIS LEG. HE TURNED BLUE AND DIED INSTANTLY.

2. A gathering of people, in this case for prayer.

THE END

Murad Kangal

1. One ser is equal to about 840 gms.

MURAD WALKED BACK HOME WITH A HEAVY HEART. BUT HE QUICKENED HIS STEPS AT THE THOUGHT OF HIS WAITING GUESTS.
ON REACHING HOME...
KANGALNI, I HAVE PAWNED YUSUF. LOOK HERE'S THE *SER* OF RICE. NOW JUST START COOKING.
MEANWHILE MANIK PIR SAW ALL THIS DRAMA TAKING PLACE. HE CALLED ON GODDESS LAKSHMI...
OH, MA LAKHI, GODDESS OF WEALTH, HELP THIS POOR MAN MURAD. VISIT HIS LITTLE HUT AND COOK HIS FOOD.
HAI ALLAH, WHERE DID ALL THIS FOOD COME FROM!
QUICK! THERE'S NO TIME TO THINK. JUST SERVE OUR GUESTS!
IN A MOMENT LAKSHMI PREPARED FIVE DISHES INCLUDING FISH CURRY...
WHY ONLY TWO LEAVES?
WE, ER....UMMM...CAN EAT LATER. WHY DON'T YOU START?

2. A musical festival. 3. Single string instrument.

THE END

The Dreamers
ONE DAY GOPAL BHAR OVERHEARD HIS NEIGHBOURS ENGAGED IN AN UNUSUAL EXCHANGE.
WHEN I GET SOME MONEY, RAZIA, I AM GOING TO BUY A COW.
HAN HAN RAFIQ MIYAN, THEN I WILL MILK THE COW. WE WILL NEED LOTS OF POTS. I WILL HAVE TO GO AND BUY SOME.
NEXT DAY..
WHAT DID YOU BUY RAZIA?
OH, POTS. ONE FOR MILK, ONE FOR BUTTERMILK, ONE FOR BUTTER, ONE FOR GHEE.
THAT'S NICE, BUT WHAT ABOUT THE FIFTH ONE?
THAT'S FOR CARRYING SOME OF OUR EXTRA MILK TO MY SISTER.
WHAT! CARRY MILK TO YOUR SISTER? HOW LONG HAVE YOU BEEN DOING THAT?
HE GRABBED THE POTS AND ...
CRACK!
SPLAT!
I AM THE ONE WHO TAKES CARE OF THE COW AND MILKS IT. I WILL DO WHAT I WISH WITH THE EXTRA MILK.
YOU SLUT! I WORK AND SWEAT ALL DAY AND BUY A COW, AND YOU GIVE AWAY THE MILK TO YOUR SISTER? I WILL KILL YOU FIRST!!
SMASH!
PICHAAD!
UURR!
?

THIS STORY HAS BEEN ADAPTED FROM *FOLKTALES FROM INDIA* BY A.K RAMANUJAN, PUBLISHED BY PENGUIN BOOKS

THE END

Banbibi
BERAHIM AND HIS WIFE PHULBIBI DID NOT HAVE ANY CHILDREN. BERAHIM WENT TO MEDINA TO THE GRAVE OF RASUL TO PRAY FOR A CHILD.
SUDDENLY....
YOU WILL HAVE CHILDREN, MY SON, BUT NOT FROM YOUR PRESENT WIFE. GO AND GET MARRIED ONCE AGAIN AND ALLAH WILL GIVE YOU TWO BEAUTIFUL CHILDREN.
RASUL?
BERAHIM WENT BACK AND MARRIED A WOMAN CALLED GULAL AND BROUGHT HER HOME.
?
AT HOME, PHULBIBI WAS CONSUMED WITH JEALOUSY WHEN SHE HEARD THAT GULAL HAD BECOME PREGNANT.
DOES SHE THINK SHE IS AS FERTILE AS THE MANGROVE FIELDS? I MUST FIND A WAY TO GET RID OF THIS WOMAN!
ONE DAY WHEN GULAL WAS AWAY...
PHULBIBI, SUCH DELICIOUS FISH CURRY YOU'VE NEVER COOKED BEFORE! THERE IS MAGIC IN YOUR HANDS!
THAT'S ALL VERY WELL. BUT YOU SEEM TO HAVE FORGOTTEN HOW I SERVED YOU AND YOUR FAMILY FOR SO MANY YEARS!
AND ALSO THE WISH YOU HAD GRANTED ME WHEN I SAVED YOUR MOTHER FROM SNAKE-BITE! BUT WHAT IS THE USE, YOU MEN ARE ALL THE SAME, SELFISH. ***ALLAH, HOW CAN I COMPETE WITH A YOUNG WOMAN!***
ASK ME FOR ANYTHING PHULBIBI MY DEAR, ***ANYTHING!*** I HAVEN'T FORGOTTEN THE WISH!
THEN SEND GULAL TO THE FOREST AND ASK HER NEVER TO COME BACK TO THIS HOUSE!
HAI ALLAH! ***WHAT ARE YOU SAYING BIBI!*** GULAL IS GOING TO BE THE MOTHER OF MY CHILDREN!
BUT PHUBIBI WOULDN'T BUDGE AN INCH. SO...
GULAL, LET'S GO TO THE FOREST TOMORROW TO COLLECT SOME HONEY.

NEXT DAY...
GOOD RIDDANCE! I HOPE THIS IS THE LAST TIME I SET MY EYES ON HER! HMMPH!
BERAHIM TOOK GULAL DEEPER AND DEEPER INTO THE FOREST.
IT'S GETTING LATE, SHOULDN'T WE HEAD BACK? OUR MASKS WON'T PROTECT US ANY MORE.
YES, BUT FIRST LET ME FIND SOME WATER, I'M THIRSTY.
DARKNESS FELL QUICKLY BUT THERE WAS NO SIGN OF BERAHIM.
WHERE IS HE...?
I SAW HIM WALK THIS WAY.
MIYAAAAAN!
MIYAAAAAN!
OH, I'M EXHAUSTED. LET ME REST FOR A WHILE. YAWN!
SIGH!
NEXT MORNING ....
SO THAT'S WHY HE BROUGHT ME TO THE JUNGLE, TO ABANDON ME IN THIS STATE. I WONDER WHY! SOB! SOB!
IT WASN'T LONG BEFORE GULAL WENT INTO LABOUR.
AAAAAH!
?
!

SHE GAVE BIRTH TO TWO CHILDREN, BANBIBI AND SHAHJANGULI. BUT THE JOY OF BECOMING A MOTHER WAS OVERSHADOWED BY A SENSE OF HOPELESSNESS.
HOW WILL I BRING UP TWO CHILDREN ALL BY MYSELF IN THIS WRETCHED FOREST!?
GULAL WAS WEAK AND HUNGRY. SHE PICKED UP SHAHJANGULI IN HER ARMS LEAVING BANBIBI CRYING ON A PILE OF LEAVES.
OH SPIRITS OF THE FOREST, PROTECT MY LITTLE GIRL! I'M LEAVING WITH MY SON, SHAHJAN.
?
BUT BANBIBI DIDN'T REMAIN MOTHERLESS FOR LONG. A DEER FAMILY NURTURED HER.
THE TIGER CUB, CALLED CHANCHAL WAS HER CONSTANT COMPANION.
BE CAREFUL BANBIBI DON'T SLIDE OFF!
MANY YEARS PASSED BY....
MEANWHILE... BEYOND THE FRONTIERS OF THIS DENSE FOREST, BERAHIM WAS TORMENTED BY HIS OWN CONSCIENCE. MANY A TIME HE TRIED TO GATHER ENOUGH COURAGE TO LOOK FOR HIS ABANDONED FAMILY.
I CAN'T BEAR THIS ANY LONGER, I MUST FIND HER... OH GULAL ...
THE SEARCH CONTINUED FOR DAYS.....
GULAL!
GULAL, MY LOVE! HOW DO I BEGIN? I DON'T EVEN KNOW IF I DESERVE TO BE FORGIVEN. BUT PLEASE GIVE ME ONE MORE CHANCE!

1. The Sunderbans.

2. King of the South, also known as Lord of Tigers. 3. The muslim call to prayer. 4. Dakshin Ray's mother.

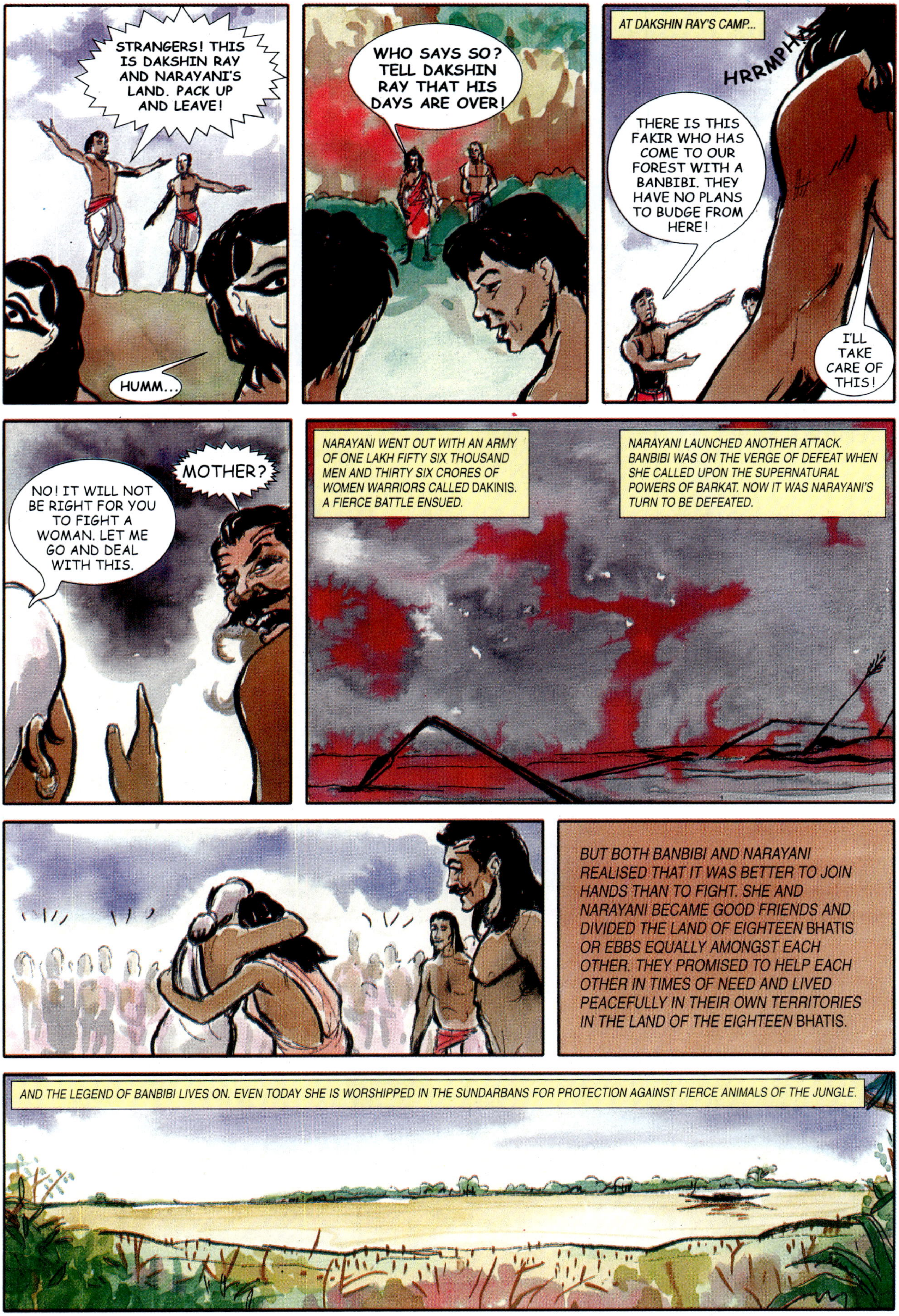

STRANGERS! THIS IS DAKSHIN RAY AND NARAYANI'S LAND. PACK UP AND LEAVE!
HUMM...
WHO SAYS SO? TELL DAKSHIN RAY THAT HIS DAYS ARE OVER!
AT DAKSHIN RAY'S CAMP...
HRRMPH
THERE IS THIS FAKIR WHO HAS COME TO OUR FOREST WITH A BANBIBI. THEY HAVE NO PLANS TO BUDGE FROM HERE!
I'LL TAKE CARE OF THIS!
MOTHER?
NO! IT WILL NOT BE RIGHT FOR YOU TO FIGHT A WOMAN. LET ME GO AND DEAL WITH THIS.
NARAYANI WENT OUT WITH AN ARMY OF ONE LAKH FIFTY SIX THOUSAND MEN AND THIRTY SIX CRORES OF WOMEN WARRIORS CALLED DAKINIS. A FIERCE BATTLE ENSUED.
NARAYANI LAUNCHED ANOTHER ATTACK. BANBIBI WAS ON THE VERGE OF DEFEAT WHEN SHE CALLED UPON THE SUPERNATURAL POWERS OF BARKAT. NOW IT WAS NARAYANI'S TURN TO BE DEFEATED.
BUT BOTH BANBIBI AND NARAYANI REALISED THAT IT WAS BETTER TO JOIN HANDS THAN TO FIGHT. SHE AND NARAYANI BECAME GOOD FRIENDS AND DIVIDED THE LAND OF EIGHTEEN BHATIS OR EBBS EQUALLY AMONGST EACH OTHER. THEY PROMISED TO HELP EACH OTHER IN TIMES OF NEED AND LIVED PEACEFULLY IN THEIR OWN TERRITORIES IN THE LAND OF THE EIGHTEEN BHATIS.
AND THE LEGEND OF BANBIBI LIVES ON. EVEN TODAY SHE IS WORSHIPPED IN THE SUNDARBANS FOR PROTECTION AGAINST FIERCE ANIMALS OF THE JUNGLE.

THE END

Gandharva Sen is Dead

WHEN THE KING WENT TO HIS HAREM HE WAS STILL WEEPING.
ARRE BADSHAH, WHY ARE YOU CRYING?
GANDHARVA SEN IS DEAD, RANI!
OH NO! DON'T TELL ME! POOR GANDHARVA SEN!
OOOH! SOB! SOB! OOOH!
?!?
BADSHAHZADI, WHY IS EVERYONE CRYING?
OOOH, HOO, GANDHARVA SEN IS DEAD!
WHO WAS GANDHARVA SEN TO YOUR MAJESTY? NEVER HEARD OF HIM!
COME TO THINK OF IT, I REALLY DON'T KNOW!!
WHO IS THIS GANDHARVA SEN THAT YOU ARE ALL LAMENTING ABOUT?
UH! UH!??
GULP!

THE BADSHAH WALKED BRISKLY DOWN THE CORRIDOR THAT LED TO THE COURT.
ARRE BABA! WHAT A QUESTION...WHAT A QUESTION!
CLUCK CLUCK!
MAHAMANTRI, ER...WHO EXACTLY WAS THIS GANDHARVA SEN?
UH...MMM... FRANKLY HUZOOR, I HAVE NO IDEA, PARDON ME.
I SAW THE SENAPATI CRYING, SAYING THAT GANDHARAVA SEN IS DEAD, SO I TOO CRIED TO GIVE HIM COMPANY.
YOU ARE A FOOL! GO AT ONCE AND FIND OUT WHO GANDHARVA SEN WAS!
THE MINISTER RAN TO LOOK FOR THE SENAPATI.
SENAPATI, WHO WAS GANDHARVA SEN? YOU MUST SURELY KNOW, EH.
SOB
I'M AFRAID....
...I DON'T HAVE THE SLIGHTEST IDEA. BINOO, THE JAMADAR CAME CRYING, SAYING THAT GANDHARVA SEN WAS DEAD, SO I TOO WEPT IN ORDER TO KEEP HIM COMPANY.
BINOO WAS CLEANING OUT THE DRAINS BEHIND THE PALACE. HIS SHOULDERS WERE SHAKING WITH GRIEF.
BINOO, O BINOO! WHO WAS THIS GANDHARVA SEN YOU TOLD ME ABOUT?
I DON'T KNOW HUZOOR.
I SAW MY WIFE WEEPING OVER THE DEATH OF GANDHARVA SEN. I FELT SORRY FOR HER AND CAME TO YOU TO REPORT IT. I CRIED BECAUSE MY WIFE WAS CRYING.

1. Death is me!

THE END

Bada Khan Ghazi
AFTER TRAVELLING THROUGH THE HEAT AND HUMIDITY OF THE SUNDARBANS FOR A MONTH, BADA KHAN GHAZI AND KALU MIAN DECIDED TO CAMP IN THE VILLAGE OF CHANDIPUR UNDER THE COOL SHADE OF A SHEORAH TREE.
?
SO COOL DOWN HERE!
THAT DAY HAPPENED TO BE THE AUSPICIOUS DAY OF THE BARUNI SNAN WHEN PEOPLE TAKE A HOLY DIP IN THE RIVER ADIGANGA. SUDDENLY...
LOOK AT THE FAKIR SITTING UNDER THE TREE!
HUH...UH! THIS IS NO ORDINARY FAKIR!
SUCH BEAUTY! COULD I BE DREAMING? WHO IS SHE?
KALU MIAN, WAKE UP!
WAKE UP I SAY! I HAVE JUST SEEN THE MOST BEAUTIFUL WOMAN IN THIS WORLD! LOOK, SHE'S WALKING TOWARDS THE GHATS. GO, FIND OUT WHO SHE IS!
OOO..MMMM... LET ME SLEEP ZZZZ!
ACCOMPANIED BY HER MAIDS, THE BEAUTIFUL PRINCESS REACHED THE GHATS FOR A HOLY DIP.
SPLASH
SPLASH

ZZZ...I AM NOT GOING ANYWHERE! ASKING ABOUT SOME STUPID WOMAN FORGET IT! ZZZZ
FORGET IT? LISTEN, MIAN YOU DON'T KNOW WHAT IT IS LIKE TO BE BLESSED BY SUCH AN APPARITION!
sSSNORE!
FIND OUT WHO SHE IS. IS SHE MARRIED? DON'T LET HER GET AWAY!
I WAS SEEING SUCH A WONDERFUL DREAM! MMPH... LET'S SEE WHAT I CAN DO...
YAWN!
STRETCH!
HURRY!
COME ON, KALU MIAN, RISE TO THE OCCASION! BRILLIANT MIND, DON'T LET ME DOWN!
MEAN WHILE...
WHY AM I STILL THINKING ABOUT THAT FAKIR?
ALL OF A SUDDEN...
NIRLAJJ![1] GET AWAY YOU PEEPING TOM!
ER...ER...
PARDON MY INTRUSION! YOUR MISTRESS....WHO IS SHE...ER...IS SHE MARRIED?
WHY, WHY DO YOU WANT TO KNOW? BUT SINCE YOU ASK, SHE IS PRINCESS SHUBHADRA, THE DAUGHTER OF MUKUT.
AND ER.. YOUR NAME, MY LADY?
CHANDRA, THE PRINCESS'S MAID IN WAITING.
MY LADY, LET'S HEAD BACK. THIS PLACE IS...
FORGET ABOUT HER! SHE IS THE PRINCESS OF KHANIYA, THE DAUGHTER OF A BRAHMIN KING! SHE'S ENTIRELY OUT OF BOUNDS FOR YOU! I MIGHT HAVE BETTER LUCK THOUGH. HER MAID HAS ALREADY CRUMBLED BEFORE MY CHARMS.
UNDER THE TREE...
HOW INSENSITIVE! DO YOU HAVE THE SLIGHTEST IDEA WHAT I'M GOING THROUGH? ANYHOW, REMEMBER YOUR DUTY. FIND A WAY TO ARRANGE AN ALLIANCE BETWEEN THE PRINCESS AND MYSELF.
YOU HAVE NEVER SPOKEN TO ME LIKE THIS BEFORE! GASP!
COME, COME IT'S ALRIGHT! FORGIVE ME, I SPOKE SHARPLY. I'M NOT MYSELF SINCE I SET EYES ON THAT GIRL. WITHOUT HER I WILL NOT LIVE AND WHO KNOWS, IN MY DESTRUCTION MAY LIE THE DESTRUCTION OF ALL INNOCENCE. GO NEGOTIATE WITH THE KING!

1. Shameless.

HOW WILL I NEGOTIATE FOR A HINDU BRIDE FOR MY MUSLIM MASTER, AND THAT TOO, DAUGHTER OF A BRAHMIN KING?!
SCRATCH SCRATCH
SO AS THEY SAY, ALL IS FAIR IN LOVE AND WAR. KALU MIAN DRESSED AS A BRAHMIN, WENT TOWARDS THE PALACE GATES OF KHANIYA.
AT THE PALACE GATE...
NOT FOR ALMS! THIS PUROHIT 2 HAS COME ALL THE WAY TO SEE THE KING!
PRANAM MAHARAJ! I HAVE BROUGHT YOU AN EXCELLENT PROPOSAL FOR PRINCESS SHUBHADRA. I AM HERE TO REPRESENT THE GREAT BADA KHAN GHAZI, ILLUSTRIOUS KING, AND ABSOLUTE MONARCH OF THE LOWER PROVINCES AND HEIR TO SIKANDER SHAH!
GULP!
HE IS ONE OF THE THE MOST LEARNED BRAHMINS OF THE REGION.
GHAZI???
AND HAVING HEARD ABOUT THIS REMARKABLE MAN, WOULD THE EQUALLY NOBLE KING ACCEPT HIM AS HIS SON-IN-LAW?
I'M AFRAID I HAVE NEVER HEARD ABOUT THIS KING WHOSE PRAISES YOU SING. BUT SINCE YOU HAVE COME ALL THE WAY....
RAMBEDHO! PLEASE SEE TO IT THAT OUR GUEST IS FED PROPERLY, AS BEFITTING A WORTHY BRAHMIN!
??? GHAZI?
TAP!
TAP!
AH FOOD! THE BEST WAY TO ROUND OFF THIS MEAL WOULD BE A GLIMPSE OF CHANDRA!
SOMETHING ODD ABOUT THIS BRAHMIN!

2. Priest.

LEARNED MEN, MY PANDITS, REFER TO EVERY POSSIBLE SCRIPTURE AND TELL ME IF 'GHAZI' IS A BRAHMIN NAME. QUICK! I MUST CONVEY MY DECISION SOON!
GHAZI??
??
GHAZI??
GHAZI! GHAZI! GHAZI!
GHAZI! GHAZI! GHAZI!
SUDDENLY.....
THE MAN IS AN IMPOSTOR, MAHARAJ! I WILL LAY A WAGER THAT THERE IS NOT A SINGLE BRAHMIN "GHAZI" IN THE WHOLE WORLD!
IMPOSTER!
FRAUD!
WHAT!
DRAG THIS MAN THROUGH THE PALACE BY HIS NECK AND THROW HIM ON THE STREETS!
KALU MIAN RAN FOR HIS LIFE.
SCRAM!

3. Just saved myself!

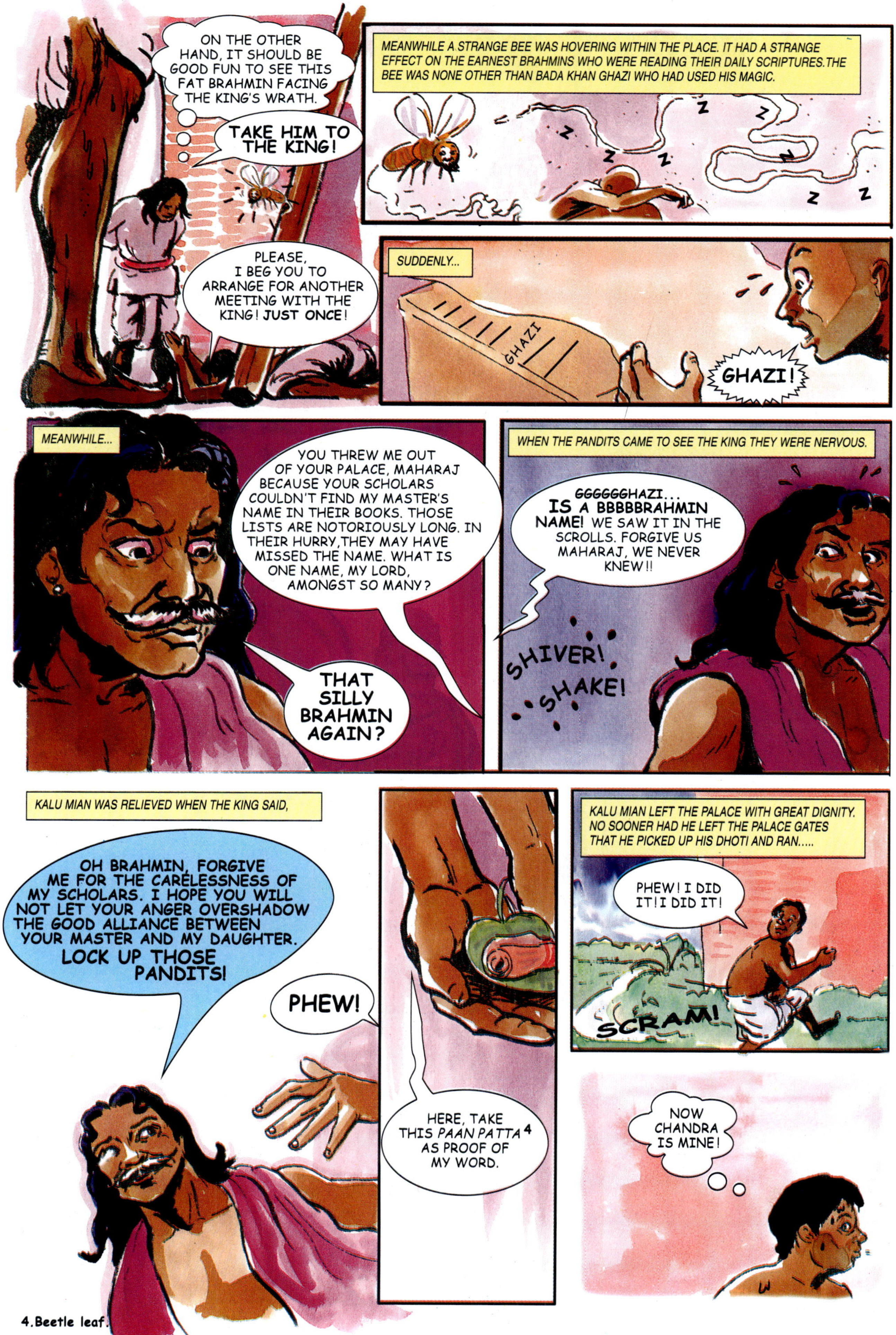

4.Beetle leaf.

5. Groom's party

6. A dalit community from Bengal.

BADA KHAN GHAZI WAS ASTONISHED...
CHICKEN! HOW ON EARTH WILL YOU GO TO A BRAHMIN'S HOUSE WITH THAT?
JUST WAIT AND SEE!
ON THE DAY OF THE WEDDING, A PROCESSION OF BAAGHS DISGUISED AS BRAHMINS FOLLOWED BADA KHAN GHAZI AND KALU MIAN TO KHANIYA.
HERE COME THE BARJATRIS!
AT THE CAMP JUST BEFORE THE WEDDING, KALU MIAN DOLED OUT THE CHICKEN TO THE BAAGHS AND THEY POLISHED IT ALL OFF.
BELCH!
BURP!
SLURP!
AS USUAL RAMBHEDO WAS SNOOPING AROUND...
SOMETHING STRANGE ABOUT THESE BARJATRIS? I CAN SMELL SOMETHING.
SNIFF!
EH! WHAT'S THIS? SHORBONASH!7 IF THIS IS NOT CHICKEN MEAT! I'LL BE DAMNED! KNEW IT! BRAHMINS INDEED!
STOP THE WEDDING!!
WHAT!
STOP!
FIND OUT WHO THEY ARE, THESE TRICKSTERS!
LINE THEM UP AND STRIP THEM ONE BY ONE!
FLOG THESE LOWER CASTE MENIALS!
THE BARJATRIS FLED TOWARDS THE SHEORAH TREE.
RUN!

7. Damnation!

ANGERED BEYOND CONTROL AND OVERCOME BY LOVE FOR SHUBHADRA,
BADA KHAN GHAZI TURNED TO THE SHEORAH TREE AND...
SWOOSH!
TO KHANIYA! WAR!
A FIERCE BATTLE ENSUED IN WHICH KING MUKUT WAS VANQUISHED BY BADA KHAN GHAZI AND HIS ARMY OF BAAGHS.
KING MUKUT, ROUTED AND HUMBLED, HAD TO PAY FOR HIS FREEDOM BY GIVING AWAY HIS DAUGHTER'S HAND IN MARRIAGE! THUS BADA KHAN GHAZI, THE MUSLIM FAKIR MAGICIAN WAS MARRIED TO SHUBHADRA, THE BRAHMIN PRINCESS AND THE TWO COMMUNITIES LIVED HAPPILY EVER AFTER...
IN THE CHAOS THAT FOLLOWED RAMABEDHO'S DISCOVERY, KALU MIAN MANAGED TO SALVAGE ONE OF THE RED AND GOLD SARIS. HE NOW HAS A SMALL HOUSE. CHANDRA SOMETIMES SPREADS THE RED AND GOLD SARI ON THEIR FLOOR, MAKING BELIEVE IT IS A MAP OF THE WORLD. THEY SLEEP THROUGH THE AFTERNOON HEAT....

God is Everywhere

1. A local market

ANINDO REMEMBERED HIS GURU'S WORDS...
GOD IS EVERYWHERE... HE DWELLS...
ARE YOU DEAF? I AM THE MAHOUT AND I SAY THAT THIS ELEPHANT IS MAD! GET OUT OF THE WAY IF YOU DON'T WANT TO DIE!
WHY SHOULD I RUN? GOD IS IN THIS ELEPHANT TOO, AS HE IS IN ME.
HOW CAN GOD HURT GOD...
BUT THEN...
HELP HELP GOD!
AMAKE² BACHAO!
TWOOSH!

2. Save me!

OWWW!
THIS REALLY HURTS! HOW CAN GOD DO THIS TO ME?
KRACK!
ANINDO, CAN YOU HEAR ME? GET UP! WHY DIDN'T YOU MOVE WHEN YOU WERE ASKED TO?
GROAN!
YOU HAD SAID THAT GOD IS IN EVERYTHING. LOOK WHAT THE ELEPHANT DID TO ME.
HA! HA! HA! HA!
YES, IT IS TRUE THAT GOD IS IN EVERYTHING. THE ELEPHANT IS CERTAINLY GOD. BUT SO WAS THE MAHOUT TELLING YOU TO GET OUT OF THE WAY. WHY DIDN'T YOU LISTEN TO **HIM**?
HA!
HA!

THE END

1. Another name for the Sunderbans

I'LL MISS YOU MY LITTLE ONE!
GOODBYE, MY DEAR. TAKE CARE.
SOB!
POOF!
POOF!
GAURI WAS AS EXCITED AS WE ALL ARE BEFORE ANY TRAVEL. SHE DECIDED ON A LITTLE TRAVEL MAKEOVER, BUT THIS ONE IS A LITTLE DIFFICULT FOR MOST OF US! HOW MANY OF US CAN DO THIS?
POOF!
POOF!
SO, DO YOU LIKE ME THIS WAY AS A LITTLE EIGHT YEAR OLD GIRL?
IN BHATIR DESH...
THE HUMBLE FISHING VILLAGE OF KANTABENIYA.
SHANTY HUTS AND EMACIATED PEOPLE. SO MUCH RICHNESS OF NATURE AND SO MUCH POVERTY AT THE SAME TIME! I GUESS I AM RESPONSIBLE FOR BOTH. **GULP**!
GUESS THIS IS WHERE I MUST STOP AND DO SOMETHING. MY ADVENTURE STARTS **NOW**!

BUT, BUT...WHY IS NO ONE BOTHERED ABOUT ME IN THIS VILLAGE? AREN'T THEY SURPRISED TO SEE A LITTLE GIRL WANDERING ABOUT?
AH ,THERE'S A FISHERMAN. GUESS I'LL HAVE TO GET HIS ATTENTION SOMEHOW!
TINKLE!
TINKLE!
WHO ARE YOU? WHAT ARE YOU DOING HERE IN KANTABENIYA? WHERE ARE YOUR PARENTS?
THEY ARE WAY UP THERE! TEE HEE!
BABA, I'M AS LOST AS A NEEDLE IN A HAYSTACK! CAN I COME HOME WITH YOU?
HA! HOME? IS IT A ***HOME*** WHERE PEOPLE ARE STARVING? MY WIFE TUMPA HASN'T EATEN IN TWO DAYS. HOW CAN I FEED ***YOU***?
PLEASE BABA, GIVE ME A MORSEL, THAT'S ALL. I TOO HAVEN'T EATEN IN THREE DAYS.
HRRMPH! YOU KIDS ARE IMPOSSIBLE, TUGGING AT A POOR MAN'S HEART. COME LET ME SEE WHAT I CAN DO.
TUMPA WAS WAITING FOR HER HUSBAND...

2.Bengali New Year 3.Pumpkin

4. Little girl **5.** A coconut sweet **6.** A sweet made of rice and milk.

MEANWHILE THE-COMMANDER-IN-CHIEF OF KING SHOVA SINGHA, THE KING OF MAHISHADAL WAS ON A TOUR OF THE REGION AND SAW THE PROSPEROUS VILLAGE FROM THE BOAT.
DAS BABU, HAVE YOU SEEN THAT VILLAGE ACROSS THE RIVER? ISN'T IT MORE PROSPEROUS THAN ALL THE OTHER POVERTY STRICKEN VILLAGES?
LET'S FIND OUT THE SECRET BEHIND THEIR PROSPERITY! WHAT SHOULD WE DO?
SIR, DISGUISE YOURSELF AND WALK AROUND THE VILLAGE. THAT WAY YOU CAN GET ALL THE LOCAL GOSSIP.
DRESSED AS A SAUDAGAR[7], THE GENERAL WANDERED THE STREETS OF KANTABENIYA.
WE'RE SO LUCKY!
WHAT WILL WE DO WITHOUT HER?
GOD BLESS OUR LITTLE *KHUKI*!
???
SHE IS THE REAL DAUGHTER OF THIS VILLAGE.
BACK AT THE PALACE...
MAHARAJ, THE SECRET OF KANTABENIYA'S PROSPERITY IS A LITTLE GIRL WHO SEEMS TO HAVE APPEARED FROM NOWHERE!
A LITTLE GIRL! **PREPOSTEROUS!** SO WHAT STOPS YOU SENAPATI? IF SHE CAN ENDOW A WRETCHED VILLAGE WITH SO MUCH WEALTH, WHY CAN'T **WE** GET HER FOR MAHISHADAL? **GO GET HER!** MOBILISE THE ARMY, TERRORISE THE VILLAGERS! I GIVE YOU FULL POWERS!

7. Merchant.

ON REACHING THE SHORES OF KANTABENIYA...
MEN! DO YOU HEAR ME? LOOK IN EVERY CORNER OF THE VILLAGE! LEAVE NO STONE UNTURNED. GET THE GIRL! THAT'S AN ORDER!
THE ARMY TURNED THE VILLAGE UPSIDE DOWN.
SHE IS NOT HERE!
NOT HERE!
NOT HERE EITHER!
THAT LITTLE RASCAL OF A GIRL! DOES SHE THINK SHE CAN HIDE FOR LONG?
GET THAT OLD FISHERMAN. THRASH HIM WITHIN AN INCH OF HIS LIFE! IF HE DOESN'T SPEAK GET THE NEXT AND THE NEXT. IF NOTHING WORKS, START WITH THE WOMEN AND CHILDREN! HURRY!
GOOD GRIEF!
HERE HE IS, SARKAR, BUT HE REFUSES TO SPEAK.
THRASH HIM, AND HE WILL!
STOP! STOP TORTURING THIS MAN. I'M THE ONE YOU ARE LOOKING FOR! TAKE ME INSTEAD!
THE GIRL! GET HER BEFORE SHE GIVES US THE SLIP AGAIN.

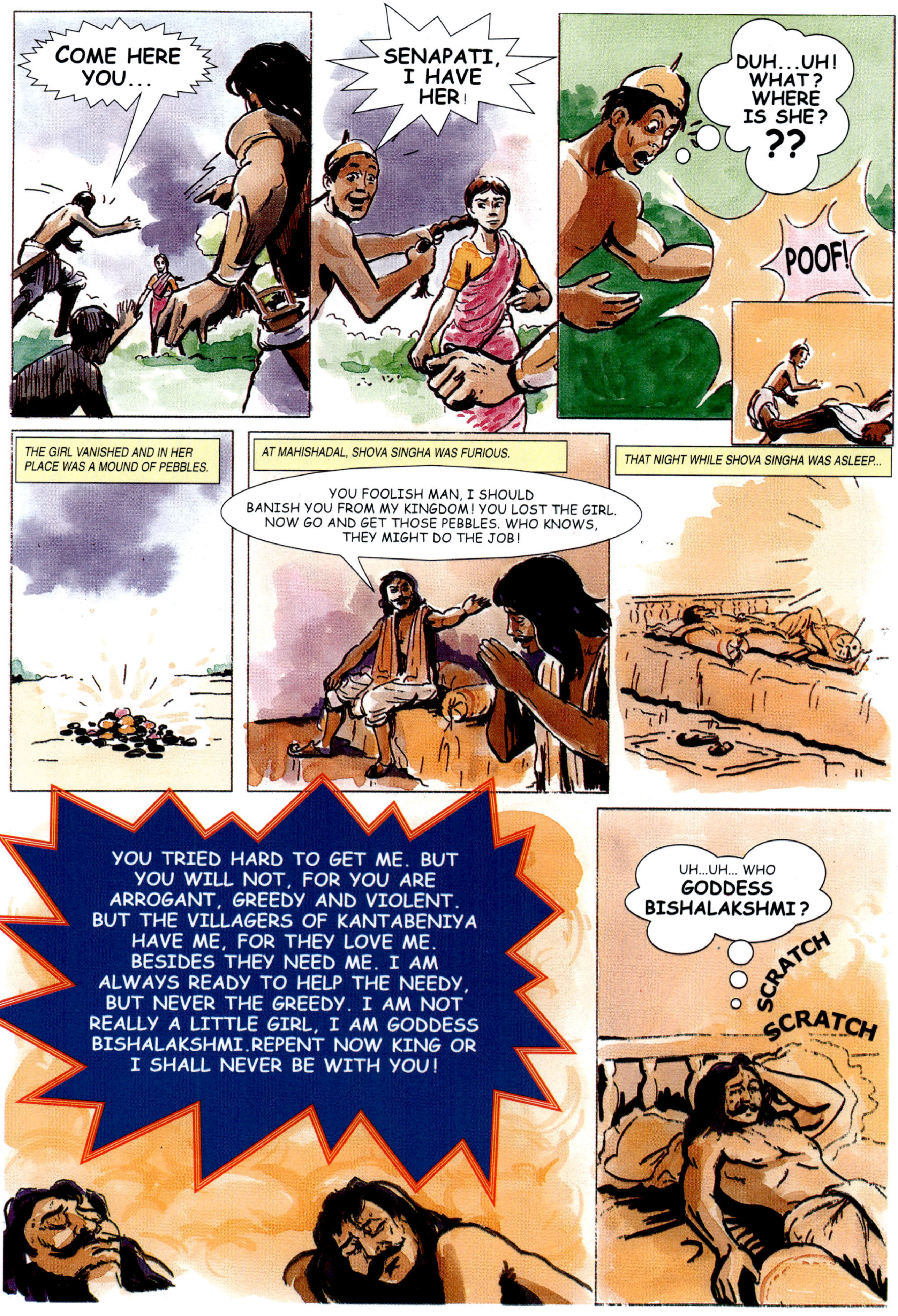

COME HERE YOU...
SENAPATI, I HAVE HER!
DUH...UH! WHAT? WHERE IS SHE? ??
POOF!
THE GIRL VANISHED AND IN HER PLACE WAS A MOUND OF PEBBLES.
AT MAHISHADAL, SHOVA SINGHA WAS FURIOUS.
YOU FOOLISH MAN, I SHOULD BANISH YOU FROM MY KINGDOM! YOU LOST THE GIRL. NOW GO AND GET THOSE PEBBLES. WHO KNOWS, THEY MIGHT DO THE JOB!
THAT NIGHT WHILE SHOVA SINGHA WAS ASLEEP...
YOU TRIED HARD TO GET ME. BUT YOU WILL NOT, FOR YOU ARE ARROGANT, GREEDY AND VIOLENT. BUT THE VILLAGERS OF KANTABENIYA HAVE ME, FOR THEY LOVE ME. BESIDES THEY NEED ME. I AM ALWAYS READY TO HELP THE NEEDY, BUT NEVER THE GREEDY. I AM NOT REALLY A LITTLE GIRL, I AM GODDESS BISHALAKSHMI. REPENT NOW KING OR I SHALL NEVER BE WITH YOU!
UH...UH... WHO GODDESS BISHALAKSHMI?
SCRATCH
SCRATCH

MEAN WHILE THE VILLAGERS STARED SADLY AT THE MOUND OF PEBBLES.
SUDDENLY...
MY WONDERFUL FRIENDS, I AM THE LITTLE GIRL YOU HAVE LOVED LIKE A DAUGHTER. CALL ON ME WHENEVER YOU NEED ME. FROM NOW ON, I WILL BE KNOWN AS BISHALAKSHMI OF KANTABENIYA.
NOW YOU MUST PROTECT ME FROM THE CLUTCHES OF SHOVA SINGHA. SUBMERGE ME IN THE RIVER BEFORE HE REACHES HERE.
AND BEFORE THE VILLAGERS COULD BLINK, SHE TURNED HERSELF INTO AN IMAGE WHICH THEY CARRIED INTO THE WATER.
HURRY, I CAN SEE THE KING'S BOAT! SUBMERGE SUB....!!!
WE ARE ALMOST THERE! BUT WHAT ARE THE VILLAGERS DOING AT THE RIVER BANK?
BISHALAKSHMI, WHY HAVE YOU FORSAKEN ME? SHOW YOURSELF TO ME JUST ONCE!
JUST ONCE!
THERE, WASN'T THAT A LOVELY ADVENTURE? WHAT NEXT?

THE END

1. The three dimensional image of a deity.

DON'T BE SILLY! WHERE IS HER TONGUE?! IT'S DURGA!
IT'S KALI RE!
NO IT ISN'T.WHERE ARE ALL HER ARMS? IT'S SARASWATI.
WHY ARGUE? LET'S ASK OUR ELDERS.
IT'S GETTING DARK. LET'S HURRY! JUST BE GENTLE AND KEEP THE IMAGE IN THE CORNER BY THE FOLDED ROPES.
JUST BEFORE THEY PARTED WAYS, THEY SAT IN A CIRCLE ...
PASS ME SOME MORE!
OUR CHAMPA SERVES THE BEST HADIYA2 IN THIS REGION!
GLUG GLUG!
HNNH!
MAJHI RE MAJHI
ANANTA WAS SO TIRED THAT HE FELL INTO A DEEP SLEEP.
ZZZZZZZZZ
RRH! RRH!
IN THE WEE HOURS OF THE MORNING, ANANTA BEGAN TO DROWN... DROWN...DROWN... IN A DEAFENING SWIRL OF DHOL BEATS....
DHAK
DHAK
DHAK
SUDDENLY
DHAK
DHAK
GOOD MAN, I HATE TO DISTURB AN HONEST MAN'S SLEEP. BUT I HAD NO CHOICE. I AM BISHALAKSHMI WHOM YOU LOVE. BUT SO FAR YOU HAVE HAD NO IMAGE TO WORSHIP ME WITH. I LIVE IN THAT STONE STATUE WHICH LIES AMONG THE ROPES AT THE BOTTOM OF THE BOAT. TAKE ME AND KEEP ME IN A HUT THATCHED WITH LEAVES. THAT WILL BE MY GRANDEST TEMPLE. OFFER ME THINGS THAT ARE MOST PRECIOUS TO YOU. AND THIS VILLAGE WILL HAVE ONLY GOOD FORTUNE!
UH...DUH... DEVI BISHALAKSHMI?!
BLINK!

2.Rice beer

3. Scriptures or tenets.

AS A BRAHMIN, I'LL SIMPLY NOT ALLOW THIS! I AM GOING TO TAKE THE IDOL TO BANSHBERIYA! WHAT YOU ARE DOING IS WRONG!
HMMPH!
THERE IS NO RIGHT OR WRONG IN WORSHIP. WHAT WE OFFER HER IS OUR PRIVATE GIFT TO THE GODDESS.
WHAT IS IMPORTANT IS THE ATTITUDE WE OFFER IT WITH. WE DON'T COME TO YOUR VILLAGE AND THREATEN
TO TAKE AWAY YOUR CHANDI GODDESS, SO WHY DON'T YOU LEAVE US ALONE? WHO SAYS ONLY YOUR *SHASTRAS* ARE THE MOST WISE? WE 'LL DO WHAT WE LIKE.
ABSURD! PREPOSTEROUS!
THE ARGUMENT WAS BITTER AND HEATED AND COULD HAVE EASILY TURNED INTO A PHYSICAL FIGHT, BUT. A VILLAGE ELDER STEPPED IN.
STOP FIGHTING IN THE NAME OF RELIGION! WHY DON'T YOU NEGOTIATE AND ARRIVE AT A COMPROMISE? STOP! STOP!
HAI! HAI!
HAI! HAI!
WE ARE NOT READY TO GIVE UP THE GODDESS. SHE BELONGS TO US.
WAIT A MINUTE! I AM YOUR ZAMINDAR, A BRAHMIN. DO NOT FIGHT WITH ME. I WILL KEEP YOUR GODDESS IN MY GRAND TEMPLE AND WORSHIP HER DAILY. SHE WILL NOT BE NEGLECTED.
WE ARE FISHERMEN AND HAVE TO EARN OUR LIVELIHOOD. THEREFORE, WE SOMETIMES FAIL TO KEEP THE GODDESS IN THE CLEANEST OF SURROUNDINGS.
WE CANNOT AFFORD TO BUILD HER A GRAND TEMPLE. SO GIVING HER TO YOU DOESN'T SEEM SUCH A BAD IDEA AFTER ALL.BUT ONLY...I REPEAT, ONLY ON CERTAIN CONDITIONS.
ANANTA PAUSED AND THOUGHT HARD.
SPEAK YOUR MIND!
FIRSTLY, YOU WILL HAVE TO ARRANGE A FESTIVAL AND SPECIAL WORSHIP FOR OUR BELOVED GODDESS BISHALAKSHMI ON THE LAST TUESDAY OF THE MONTH OF VAISHAKH. ON THAT DAY, WE FISHERMEN WILL MAKE THE FIRST OFFERING. SECONDLY, MEMBERS OF ALL COMMUNITIES, IRRESPECTIVE OF CASTE, SHOULD BE ALLOWED INTO YOUR TEMPLE WHENEVER THEY WISH.
YOU HAVE MY WORD.
THERE GOES OUR BELOVED GODDESS!
NARENDRANATH TOOK THE IMAGE TO HIS VILLAGE.
PEOPLE FROM ALL CASTES AND COMMUNITIES THRONGED THE TEMPLE. THE FISHERFOLK CAME REGULARLY TO OFFER WORSHIP.

4. What damnation 5. No, it's closed for me!

6. Oh! Sure!

THE END

Songs, proverbs & riddles of the Sunderbans

The Last Cowrie

All you boys if you wish
    we could go and catch some fish
And if the fish do sting
    We'll go on the pallanquin
Ooh, my feet! These 'fish' do sting
    I'll have to take the pallanquin
Six hundred cowries for the litter?
    I'll buy some bangles to make me better
Small shell bangles, big shell bangles
    All merrily jingle jangle
One cowrie for the *sindoor*
    And Durga goes down in the river

Saral Puti

O dove! My friend
Where is the jewel?
What fish shall I catch?
Saral Puti ?
What will slice it?
A broken chopper!
In what do I cook it?
A cracked pot!
What will you serve your pa-in-law?
A big fish head!
What will you serve your ma-in -law?
Fish tail!
What will you serve your husband?
Fat fish slices!
What will the cat have?
Fish bones!
What will your son eat?
Milk and rice!
What will you eat?
Gravy and rice!

Background: This is a little rhyme which is narrated by a girl and shows how cowrie shells were used as a medium of exchange. The poem moves logically from incident to incident — first, the girl s foot is hurt which makes her dream of travelling in a palanquin, but then the palanquin costs six hundred cowries, so she abandons that idea and focuses on something more affordable like shell bangles. Now, all she is left with is one last cowrie, which can only buy her a little vermillion. Notice how the simple fishing villagers are not devoid of their own dreams, but have learnt the art of swallowing their frustration and being happy by focusing on what is within their reach. The last two lines draw their imagery from the statue of the Goddess which is immersed after the Durga puja and is used to evoke humour.

Explanation: This rhyme belongs to the domestic domain, sung by a woman. It s interesting to see how she draws a clear picture of domestic heirarchy as is familiar to her. Notice how she distributes the fish among her family members, with her getting no fish at all. Almost all of it is consumed by her in-laws with her husband getting the fattest slice of all!

Shri Pancham Pakha

Shri five is a fan
Hold it in front of your face
Six is just the shape
Seven makes the blue hyacinth dance
Eight sits on the riverbank
A pair shows up at ten
Lonely one forms eleven
Shutter at twelve is shut
Side parting for thirteen's haircut
A silver betel box has fourteen
Folded betel leaf for fifteen
Sixteen opens the door
Seventeen covers the floor
Eighteen is busy splitting cane
Nineteen is sad and in pain
At twenty the shutter closes again

Background: The rhyme *Sri Pancham Pakha* combines imagery, memory and action. This rhyme is a part of the 24 Parganas rich tradition of long rhymes. A child says this rhyme again and again as she learns to count from 5 to 20 by juggling small pieces of brick and memorises these lines. The lines themselves mean little - no logical link is established between the lines. Rather they serve up colourful little images that the child associates with each number. The images mentioned here belong to the child s immediate environment and forge a link with it.

A Feast for Twelve Hundred and Eighty

It took all of a rupee
  to buy me a *khashee**
But how do I cut and how do I share it
  My guests, they number twelve hundred eighty.

Background: This is a commonly used rhyme to teach children about the transition from cowrie shells to rupees.
4 cowries = 1 ganda
5 gandas = 20 cowries = 1 buri
4 buris = 80 cowries. = 1 pan
Later, in the era of annas, the value of 1 pan became equal to one anna.
Thus:
16 pan = 1 kahon
16 pan = 16 annas = 1 rupee
So, 1 rupee is equal to twelve hundred and eighty cowries.

* **A he-goat.**

The Deer and The Tiger

All of Bhadra it rains and rains
The deer licks the tiger's face
Watch out deer, mark my words
I'll bear it now, I'll bide my time.

Background: There is little anyone can do in the face of the forces of nature. During the torrential rains of Bhadra, even nature becomes topsy-turvy and is forced to succumb to the unusual, like the deer licking the tiger s face. What can anyone do but bide his time?

Soner gaan

Indira Gandhi passed a law
Women brought rice to Kolkata
Returned home with atta
Men could never have done it
When women begin to trade
Train fares can be saved!!

Background: This rhyme is a reflection of contemporary life. This one is sung by women, who show that they are much cleverer than men in being able to save money. The subtle indication here is that they sometimes travel without tickets! These songs are sung during the Gaajan festival and are called soner gaan.

RIDDLES

One turn to open, one to shut
A clever fakir sits under a tree
The stalk falls in his lap
While the fruit remains dangling.

Answer: Lock and key

Frisky and free at the top
Tightly tied at the bottom
The one who can't name it
Is a real ass!

Answer: A broom.